CN00827975

CARIBBEAN

David Flint

SIMON & SCHUSTER
YOUNG BOOKS

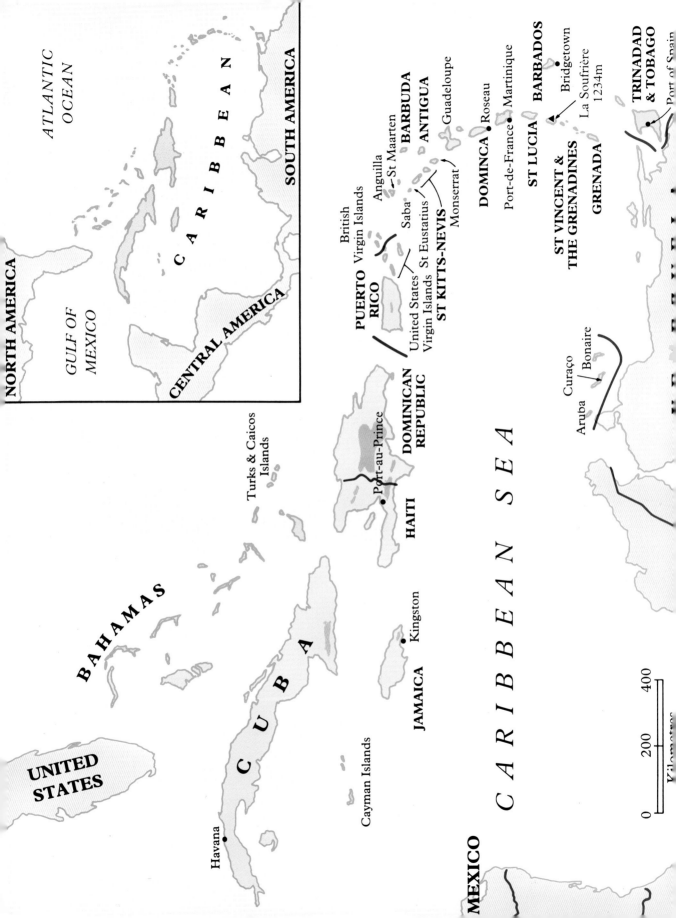

Contents

Island countries

There are thousands of islands stretched out across the Caribbean Sea between North and South America. These are the Caribbean Islands, home to 35 million people.

The islands are very different. Some are flat while others are mountainous. Some are covered in thick, steamy rainforest, and others are dry like desert. Cuba is the largest island, but others are so tiny they do not appear on many maps.

To the north of the Caribbean is the United States of America. To the west is Mexico and Central America, and the to the south countries like Venezuela in South America. To the east lies the Atlantic Ocean.

Have you visited an island? Was it flat or mountainous? Was it hot or cold?

St Lucia is a favourite stop for ships like this cruising the Caribbean.
Trips to nearby mountains or bays are always popular.

Grenada and St Vincent are covered
in tall palm trees. Small bays and
harbours are dotted around the coast.

No two Caribbean islands are the
same. Some like Beef Island and
Guana Island, shown here, are small

The Caribbean is famous for its sandy beaches, palm trees and blue sea. This is Diamond Strand beach in Martinique.

These sharp jagged peaks of ancient volcanoes have been covered by forests on St Lucia.

Many islands are the tops of volcanoes like this one on the island of St Vincent.

Mountains, volcanoes and beaches

High mountains with steep sides are found on many of the islands. Around the coasts, there are many bays with bright, sandy beaches. The sunshine together with the beaches, the warm seas and the spectacular scenery attract tourists each year.

On the island of St Vincent, there is a volcano called La Soufrière. You can smell sulphur in the steam and smoke which rise from the crater at the top of the volcano. The word 'volcano' means 'sulphur mine' in French.

Have you been to a beach? Was it sandy or pebbly? What was the weather like?

The weather

The weather is hot for most of the year in the Caribbean, with temperatures of 25°C or more. Nights are cooler, but most people wear thin clothes all the time. The dry season is from January to June. Then, cracks open up in the baked ground and tar on streets melts in the fierce heat.

Hurricanes are one of the biggest dangers. Strong forces build up in towering black clouds bringing fierce winds and torrential rain. The strengthening winds uproot trees, overturn cars and demolish buildings. Suddenly, all goes quiet and the wind drops. This is the eye of the hurricane— but don't be fooled—as the storm moves on the tempest begins again.

Do you get storms where you live? Do the storms cause much damage?

People board up windows when a
hurricane is forecast, even though
the sun still shines.

When the storm has passed it's time
to repair the walls, windows and roofs.

The hurricane batters the coast
as it whips up the sea.

Peoples

The Caribbean is named after the ancient Crib tribe. The Caribs and Arawaks were the first peoples to live on the islands. When Columbus landed in 1492, the tribes had been living there for over 1,800 years.

Spanish invaders followed, looking for gold. They forced the islanders to work as slaves. Many died from overwork and new diseases brought by the Europeans. Later, French, English and Dutch invaders arrived.
They drove the tribes off the land, and built farms and houses. Soon, they brought slaves from Africa to work on the European farms.

Now, descendants of the Africans form the largest group on the islands. Others groups include descendants of Indian and Chinese workers, descendants of Europeans, and the few remaining Caribs and Arawaks.

The great grandparents of these banana sellers came from Africa as slaves.

This post box in Curaçao is a reminder of the island's Dutch heritage.

The Caribbean has people from many ethnic origins. This girl is at a carnival in Port-au-Prince on the island of Haiti.

Sugar cane was first grown on farms worked by slaves. Even now, the cane is still harvested by hand on some islands like Haiti.

Coffee from the Blue Mountains of Jamaica is prized all over the world. The coffee beans are picked as soon as they are ripe.

Fishing is very important in the Caribbean. Fishermen often sell their catch fresh from their boats.

Cocoa pods ripen on a tree in Jamaica. Cocoa is sold to North America and Europe.

Farming and fishing

Farming is vital to all the islands and many people grow their own food. Yams, sweet potatoes, tomatoes and plantains are grown for the family, or for sale at the local market. Other crops, like sugar, bananas and cocoa are grown for sale abroad.

Bananas are picked when they are hard and green. Refrigerated ships then carry the fruits to America or Europe where they ripen in special warehouses. Lorries take them to supermarkets and fruit shops—where we can buy them.

Fish are caught around all the islands and are sold fresh, or preserved in salt. Lobster is a delicacy in St Lucia.

What fruit grows on farms near you? Have you seen fish caught at the coast?

Natural riches

The Caribbean has many valuable minerals. Bauxite is mined on Jamaica. It earns more money for Jamaica than any other export— not surprisingly, people call it 'red gold'.

Oil from wells around Trinidad is refined on the island and has helped make it rich. The industry offers well-paid jobs which attract people from the farms to towns like Port of Spain. Now, Trinidad buys more food from other countries instead of growing its own.

Trinidad also has a huge asphalt lake. Asphalt is a thick type of oil, used to surface roads in America and Europe.

Are there mines or quarries near you? What is mined? What happens to the ground when the mining is finished?

Trinidad has the world's largest lake of asphalt which is a very thick type of oil.

Oil from Caribbean wells goes to refineries like this one on the Virgin Islands.

Bauxite mining in Jamaica. Bauxite is used to make aluminium for pots and pans which are sold all over the world

On the move

Cities on richer islands like Puerto Rico or
Trinidad are often crowded with traffic.
These islands have more cars, cheap petrol
and good roads.

On other islands, and in the countryside
where most people are farmers, it is
quieter. There are few cars, and people
walk, or ride horses or donkeys.
Buses link villages with towns and cities.

People use boats between islands like a bus
service. The boats are big enough to carry
crops to markets in the larger towns.
Most islands have a runway and small
planes also hop from island to island.

How do you travel around? Have you been
on a boat? How big was it? What was the
journey like?

Water transport between islands is very important. Ferries like this link remote places with the main islands.

In many places, people have to walk long distances to work, to school or to the markets.

The airport at St Thomas on the U.S. Virgin Islands—small planes have become a vital link between the thousands of islands.

Modern towns have many different kinds of traffic, from cars, buses and vans to motor cycles and even boats.

Tourist resorts like St Croix on the U.S. Virgin Islands provide jobs for local people in hotels and restaurants.

People who work on the land sell their goods in markets like this one on Grenada.

Some people have skilled jobs in modern industries like this oil refinery on Curaçao.

Sugar cane is unloaded at the processing factory on Barbados. The sugar is sold worldwide.

Work

In the Caribbean, three out of every five workers work on the land, the fourth works in a factory or office, and the fifth in a shop or hotel. Some people own their own land, but often their farms are small. A few huge farms, called plantations, grow bananas, sugar cane, tobacco or coffee. These are owned by rich people or often by large foreign companies.

On islands like Barbados and Puerto Rico, people work in factories which make clothes, plastics and machines.
On Trinidad, cars are assembled from kits that come from Japan. All over the Caribbean many people work in tourist hotels and restaurants.

Are there factories near you? What do they make? Do many vehicles come and go?

Going to school

Schooling is important to all the countries of the Caribbean. Parents hope their children will work hard and find a good job. Most schools are in the towns, so buses collect children from remote villages. However, some children still have an hour's walk just to reach school.

School children sometimes teach reading and writing to older people who never had the chance to go to school. In countries like Cuba, many schools have farms which are run by the pupils. Most children speak at least two languages. They use their local language and learn another such as Spanish, French or English.

What language do you speak? Do you speak more than one language? Why is it useful to speak different languages?

Friends chat during a break from lessons in a Jamaican primary school.

Most schools have a uniform like this one in St Lucia.

Leisure time

With so many beautiful beaches and such good weather, the islanders are experts at water sports like diving, windsurfing or snorkelling. But Caribbean people enjoy life in many ways, like hiking, or camping, or having friends round to dinner.

On Puerto Rico and in the Dominican Republic, American baseball is a popular sport. Football is played on most of the islands and on Puerto Rico horse racing attracts big crowds.

Cricket is the favourite on the English-speaking islands. People get very excited when islands play each other. The best players hope to join the West Indies team which plays international cricket.

Caribbean people enjoy their beautiful sandy beaches and warm blue seas.

The West Indies cricket team celebrate taking a wicket during a test match.

A cooling swim at the Dunn's River Falls on Jamaica.

On some islands, like Jamaica, water sports are enjoyed by local people.

A colourful parade in Port-de-France on the island of Martinique.

Many hours are spent preparing for the Trinidad carnival.

Carnival dances and music remind people of the first carnival—a parade of slaves celebrating their freedom.

A steel band in Bridgetown, Barbados. The instruments are made from old oil drums.

Carnival and calypso

Caribbean people love to celebrate with friends, visitors or strangers. The Trinidad carnival is the biggest celebration in the Caribbean—and one of the most magnificent spectacles in the world.
It happens each year just before Lent.
There are parades, with stunning costumes, dancing to the music of steel bands, and calypso—amusing folk songs about local events.

Not all the islands celebrate at the same time or even in the same way. Martinique's carnival begins on Ash Wednesday when people dress as black and white devils.
In the Bahamas and Jamaica parades for Junkanoo, an Arawak god, are held near Christmas.

Famous landmarks

The impressive monument to the slave
in Haiti commemorates the country's
independence in 1804.

Reconstructions of traditional
Arawak and Carib homes at Guama
on Cuba.

April 1992—the West Indies cricket team in front of the pavilion in Barbados, named after the famous Caribbean cricketer, Garfield Sobers.

Martinique is part of France and sends representatives to the French government in Paris.

Devon House, a 19th century colonial mansion in Kingston, Jamaica.

Modern workers' flats in Havana, Cuba. Over 2 million people live in the island's capital and biggest port.

Facts and figures

The Caribbean—the land and people

Population:	35 million
Largest island:	Cuba 1200 km long 100 km wide
Languages:	Spanish, French, English, Dutch, Creole and local dialects like Papiamento (a mixture of Spanish, Portuguese, English and Arawak)
Religion:	Protestant, Catholic, Rastafarian, Hindu but all are practised

Countries of the Caribbean

country	capital city (*language*)
Antigua & Barbuda	St John's (*English*)
Bahamas	Nassau (*English*)
Barbados	Bridgetown (*English*)
Cuba	Havana (*Spanish*)
Dominica	Roseau (*English, Creole*)
Dominican Republic	Santo Domingo (*Spanish, various Creoles*)
Grenada	St George's (*English, Creole*)
Haiti	Port-au-Prince (*French, Creole*)
Jamaica	Kingston (*English, Creole*)
St Kitts-Nevis	Basseterre (*English*)
St Lucia	Castries (*English, Creole*)
St Vincent & the Grenadines	Kingstown (*English*)
Trinidad & Tobago	Port of Spain (*English, Creole*)

What happened when

date	event
500 BC	Early Arawak and Carib settlers.
1492	Columbus landed on the Bahamas.
1494 ↓	Spanish, British, French and Dutch settle on various of the Caribbean Islands. Drive out the surviving Caribs and Arawaks and import slaves from Africa to work on the plantations.
1804 ↓	Slaves in St Domingue revolt against French—set up independent Haiti. Gradually slavery is abolished.
1865	Dominican Republic becomes independent followed slowly by a handful of the other islands in the Caribbean.
	Some still remain dependent territories: *Britain*—Anguilla, British Virgin Islands, Cayman Islands, Monserrat, Turks & Caicos Islands *Netherlands*—Aruba, Bonaire, Curaçao, Saba, St Eustatius, St Maarten *United States*—United States Virgin Islands.
	The following are overseas departments of *France*: Guadeloupe, Martinique.
↓	The following is associated with the *United States*: Puerto Rico.

Average temperatures in Centigrade

city and country	January	June
Roseau, Dominica (east)	18°C	30°C
Havana, Cuba (north)	10°C	26°C
Kingston, Jamaica (west)	15°C	29°C
Port of Spain, Trindad & Tobago (south)	22°C	26°C